BIG FANTASTIC EARTH

By Jen Green

Penguin
Random
House

Series Editor Deborah Lock
US Senior Editor Shannon Beatty
Editors Nishtha Kapil and Katy Lennon
Senior Designer Ann Cannings
Art Editor Kanika Kalra
Picture Researcher Deepak Negi

Producer, Pre-production Nadine King
DTP Designers Nand Kishore,
Nityanand Kumar and Anita Yadav
Managing Editor Soma B. Chowdhury
Managing Art Editor Ahlawat Gunjan
Art Director Martin Wilson

Reading Consultant
Linda B. Gambrell, Ph.D.
Subject Consultant
Maryam Sharif-Draper

First American Edition, 2016
Published in the United States by DK Publishing
345 Hudson Street, New York, New York 10014

16 17 18 19 10 9 8 7 6 5 4 3 2 1
001—288410—June/16

Copyright © 2016 Dorling Kindersley Limited
DK, a Division of Penguin Random House LLC

All rights reserved. Without limiting the rights under copyright reserved above, no part of this publication
may be reproduced, stored in, or introduced into a retrieval system, or transmitted, in any form, or by any means
(electronic, mechanical, photocopying, recording, or otherwise), without the prior written permission
of both the copyright owner and the above publisher of this book.
Published in Great Britain by Dorling Kindersley Limited.

A catalog record for this book is available from the Library of Congress.

ISBN: 978-1-4654-4412-7 (Paperback)
ISBN: 978-1-4654-4413-4 (Hardcover)

DK books are available at special discounts when purchased in bulk for sales promotions,
premiums, fund-raising, or educational use. For details, contact:
DK Publishing Special Markets,
345 Hudson Street, New York, New York 10014
SpecialSales@dk.com.

Printed and bound in China.

The publisher would like to thank the following for their kind permission to reproduce their photographs:
(Key: a-above; b-below/bottom; c-center; f-far; l-left; r-right; t-top)
4–5 Dreamstime.com: Zhanghaobeibei. **6–7 Dreamstime.com:** Zhanghaobeibei. **6 Dreamstime.com:** Atovot (cr).
Fotolia: Strezhnev Pavel (clb). **NASA:** NOAA / GSFC / Suomi NPP / VIIRS / Norman Kuring (tc). **7 Dorling Kindersley:** Staatliches Museum
fur Naturkunde Stuttgart (cra). **8 Corbis:** Desmond Boylan / Reuters. **9 Getty Images:** Mondadori. **10–11 Getty Images:** De Agostini Picture
Library. **14–15 Corbis:** Scott Smith. **16 Getty Images:** Mladen Antonov. **18–19 Dreamstime.com:** Zhanghaobeibei. **18 Corbis:** Unlisted
Images (crb). **19 Corbis:** Halfdark / fstop (crb); Sergey Orlov / Design Pics (cra); Pete Saloutos / Blend Images (cl); Robert Glusic (clb). **20–21
Dreamstime.com:** Zhanghaobeibei. **23 Corbis:** José Fuste Raga. **24–25 Corbis:** Hagenmuller Jean-François / Hemis. **26–27 Corbis:** Marc
Garanger. **28-29 Dreamstime.com:** Abrashkina Maria. **30 Corbis:** Doug Pearson / JAI. **32-33 Dreamstime.com:** Zhanghaobeibei. **33 Getty
Images:** Rob Stothard (c). **34-35 Dreamstime.com:** Zhanghaobeibei. **34 Corbis:** Paul Panayiotou (cb). **Getty Images:** Tui De Roy (c). **35
Corbis:** Paul A. Souders (cb). **Getty Images:** Majority World (c). **37 Corbis:** Herbert Kratky / imageBROKER. **38-39 Getty Images:** DEA / M. Brambilla. **40-41 Corbis:** Sandro
Vannini. **42 Corbis:** Herbert Kratky / imageBROKER. **44-45 Getty Images:** Buena Vista Images. **46-47 Corbis:** Jochen Schlenker / Robert
Harding World Imagery. **48-49 Dreamstime.com:** Zhanghaobeibei. **48 Dreamstime.com:** Eknarin Maphichai (cb). **49 Corbis:** Atlantide
Phototravel (cla). **Dreamstime.com:** Howard Sandler (cb). **53 Getty Images:** George Grossman. **54-55 Corbis:** Lou Avers / dpa. **56 Corbis:**
Dave G. Houser. **58-59 Corbis:** Reinhard Dirscherl. **60-61 Dreamstime.com:** Tortoon (Frames); Zhanghaobeibei. **60 Dreamstime.com:**
Kimberly Greenleaf (cra). **61 Corbis:** Neil Rabinowitz (ca). **Getty Images:** John Elk (cb). **62–63 Dreamstime.com:** Zhanghaobeibei. **63
Dreamstime.com:** Anagram1 (c). **64 Dreamstime.com:** Glenn Nagel (t). **64-65 Corbis:** Scott Smith. **66-67 Corbis:** Ron Watts. **68-69 Corbis:**
Gary Cook / Robert Harding World Imagery. **72-73 Dreamstime.com:** Zhanghaobeibei. **73 Corbis:** Martin Harvey (cra). **74-75 Dreamstime.
com:** Nicemonkey (c); Zhanghaobeibei. **77 Corbis:** John and Lisa Merrill. **78-79 Corbis:** Michele Falzone / JAI. **81 Corbis:** Buddy Mays. **82
Getty Images:** Bloomberg. **86-87 Dreamstime.com:** Zhanghaobeibei. **86 Corbis:** (cl). **88-89 Dreamstime.com:** Zhanghaobeibei. **90-91
Dreamstime.com:** Zhanghaobeibei. **Fotolia:** Galyna Andrushko (c). **92-93 Dreamstime.com:** Zhanghaobeibei
Endpapers: **Rough Guides:** Greg Ward. **Jacket images:** *Front:* **Dorling Kindersley:** Natural History Museum, London cr, Oxford Museum
of Natural History tr; **Getty Images:** Erin Butler tc, Terushi Sho; *Back:* **Corbis:** Gary Cook / robertharding tr;
Dorling Kindersley: Staatliches Museum fur Naturkunde Stuttgart bl.
All other images © Dorling Kindersley
For further information see: www.dkimages.com

A WORLD OF IDEAS:
SEE ALL THERE IS TO KNOW
www.dk.com

Contents

Landscape Wonders
of the World

Grand Canyon

Andes

Sahara Desert

Nile River

Rockies

Grand
Canyon

Arches
National Park

NORTH
AMERICA

Atlantic
Ocean

Pacific
Ocean

SOUTH
AMERICA

Andes

Himalayas

Mount Everest

Jungfrau, Alps

EUROPE

ASIA

Mount Everest

Himalayas

AFRICA

Nile River

Lake Victoria

Mount Kilimanjaro

Sahara Desert

Indian Ocean

AUSTRALIA

Twelve Apostles

Mount Kilimanjaro

Twelve Apostles

5

TIMELINE of the  Earth.

4.6 billion years ago
A giant cloud of dust and gas came together to form a fiery ball of molten rock—the Earth.

3.8 billion years ago
Gas from volcanic eruptions formed the atmosphere. Steam condensed to form clouds and shed rain. Rainwater formed the oceans.

390 million years ago
Fish evolved and were the first animals with backbones.

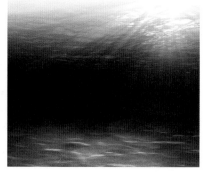

Billions of years ago

3.5 billion years ago
Life began in the oceans.

350 million years ago
The first plants appeared on land. A group of fish with fleshy fins came on land, evolving into amphibians and later, reptiles.

It has taken billions of years for the Earth to become the planet we know now. Here are some important moments from its life so far.

250 million years ago

Earth's landmasses were joined together to form one vast continent we call Pangaea.

200–145 million years ago

Pangaea slowly broke up to form smaller continents.

65 million years ago

Dinosaurs and many other animals died out, probably after an asteroid struck the Earth, causing rapid climate change.

Millions of years ago

230 million years ago

One group of reptiles evolved to become dinosaurs, the others became mammals.

6 million years ago

Humans began to evolve from a group of primates in East Africa, and later spread to other parts of Earth.

N.B. Scientists' opinions are divided on some of these dates—research into the Earth's early life is still in progress.

CHAPTER 1

HOW MOUNTAINS ARE MADE

One sunny morning in 1953, two men scrambled up a slope to a snowy summit. They hugged and then stood gazing at the incredible view spread out below. Reaching the top had not been easy—it had taken skill, organization, and great effort. The men were bundled in warm clothing to protect themselves against the intense cold. They were carrying ice axes and were roped together for safety. Both were breathing oxygen from tanks strapped to their backs.

The two climbers were Edmund Hillary from New Zealand and Tenzing Norgay, a mountain guide from Nepal. They were the first people ever to set foot on the top of Everest, the world's highest mountain. In reaching the summit, these tough adventurers triumphed where others had failed.

At 29,035 ft (8,850 m) above sea level, Everest is the highest peak in the Himalayas, in Asia. The Himalayas and neighboring mountains hold all of the world's highest peaks.

You may be surprised to hear that the rocks of these awesome peaks once lay deep under the water, on the floor of a great ocean. As proof, people hiking in the Himalayas often find the fossilized remains of sea creatures that lived at the bottom of the oceans tens of millions of years ago.

To find out how this could happen, and why some places have high mountains while others are flat, we need to understand a bit about the Earth's structure.

The ground we stand on seems hard and solid, but deep underneath the surface the rocks are red-hot—so hot that they behave like a liquid, flowing like thick syrup.

The rocks of Earth's outer layer, which is called the crust, ride on top of this red-hot, molten layer like hunks of bread in a simmering soup. The crust is not one continuous layer. Instead it is broken into sections, like a cracked eggshell. These huge slabs of rock, called tectonic plates, fit together like a globe-sized jigsaw puzzle. They lie beneath both the land and the oceans.

Driven by churning currents in the red-hot, squishy rock below, tectonic plates drift very slowly across the planet. They shift approximately an inch a year, but over the millions of years that our planet has existed, those tiny shifts add up to thousands of miles.

Everest and other peaks in the Himalayas were formed by a process called uplift. South of the Himalayas lies the large landmass of India, but India was not always part of Asia. Seventy million years ago it was a huge island carried by a plate that was inching slowly but steadily northward.

Around 50 million years ago, the plate carrying India crashed into the plate bearing Asia. This collision was slow, but the force was colossal. As the plates collided, the zone between them slowly crumpled upward to form a range of mountains— the mighty Himalayas. The pressure continues to this day, which explains why these jagged mountains are getting taller each year.

Imagine that you are holding a slab of modeling clay between your hands. If you push inward from both sides, the middle of the slab would bend upward. This is how mountains like the Himalayas formed.

   Mountains formed by plate collisions are called fold mountains, and they include many of the world's greatest mountain ranges, such as the Rockies and Andes in the Americas.

   Not all mountains are formed by uplift. Some are formed by other land disruption caused by plate movement. As these giant sections slowly drift across the world, they may scrape past one another, causing earthquakes, or they may pull apart. The separation of plates causes a weak point in the crust, which allows red-hot, molten rock from below to surge

up and spill out onto the surface. The weak point is a volcano, and when molten rock, called lava, spills out, along with billowing clouds of ash, gas, and steam, we call it an eruption. The red-hot lava that erupts from a volcano cools and hardens to form solid rock. If the eruption continues, layers of ash and lava may build up to form a steep, cone-shaped peak. Unlike fold mountains, which form ranges, volcanic peaks may be isolated and tower high above the surrounding lowlands.

Mount Kilimanjaro, Africa's highest mountain, is a dormant (inactive) volcano. This tall peak is covered with snow even though it lies on the **equator**. As Hillary and Norgay knew well, the tops of mountains are always cold because the air is thin at great heights and cannot hold as much of the sun's heat as the air at sea level.

Volcanoes erupt under oceans as well as on land. If an eruption continues on the seabed, lava builds up to form a steep, cone-shaped peak called a seamount. Eventually, so much lava may erupt that the seamount breaks the surface and becomes an island.

Many remote islands in the middle of the oceans formed in this way. The Pacific Islands of Hawaii are an example. The highest volcano on Hawaii, called Mauna Kea, stands 13,796 ft (4,205 m) above sea level. But if measured from the ocean bed, Mauna Kea rises an incredible 33,480 ft (10,205 m). That makes it the world's highest mountain—taller even than Mount Everest, which was first conquered by Hillary and Norgay on that day in 1953.

Types of Mountains

Mountains are steep-sided areas that rise at least 1,000 ft (305 m) above the surrounding land. Mountains form because of tectonic plate movement deep below the Earth's crust. Different types of mountains form in different ways.

VOLCANIC MOUNTAINS

Volcanoes form where molten rock erupts through a weak point in the crust. Layers of lava and ash build up to make a cone-shaped mountain.

BLOCK MOUNTAINS

These form where rocks shatter and develop deep cracks because of plate movement. A slab of rock may then be forced upward between cracks.

FOLD MOUNTAINS

These form where tectonic plates press together. The crust in between buckles upward into giant folds.

PLATEAU

A flat-topped area of high ground. Plateaus can form in several ways: because of volcanic eruptions, uplift, faults, or erosion.

RIFT VALLEY

This forms where a block of land slips down between faults. It forms a deep chasm with mountains on either side.

DOME MOUNTAINS

These form where molten rock wells up from below and pushes the rocks of the crust upward to form a dome.

Everest

Are you ready to take on the ultimate survival challenge?

Climbing Mount Everest will test your body to its limits.
It's an adventure that will certainly keep you on your toes!

Mount Everest has claimed the lives of many climbers
over the years. Visitors are advised to stay alert and ensure
that they are prepared for anything
on their journey to the peak.

Breathe easy

▲ Heights above 26,000 ft (8,000 m) are known as
"the death zone" because of the lack of oxygen.
All climbers should carry oxygen with them at this
altitude so that they can breathe.

Sub-zero temperatures

▲ The temperature at the summit of Mount Everest
never rises above freezing point. Wear lots of warm
layers, including gloves and a ski mask to keep you
warm and to avoid hypothermia or frostbite.

Survival Guide

Learn the ropes

▲ Make sure that you have new, strong ropes when climbing and stay clipped on whenever possible. The ice is slippery and could send you plunging to your death; make sure you use ice axes and boot spikes, called crampons, to keep your grip.

Deadly icefalls

▲ An icefall is an area where ice breaks into huge chunks, called seracs, and tumbles down the side of a mountain. Seracs are unpredictable and can crush any climber that gets in their path. Move quickly and stay alert to increase your chances of surviving an icefall.

Wait your turn

▲ Climbing Mount Everest is becoming very popular. Because of this, many of the pathways are very busy, so long lines are likely. Be aware of those around you and keep yourself warm when waiting for your turn to the top of the mountain.

CHAPTER 2

CARVED IN ICE

Ride the little train that climbs high into the Alps in Switzerland, and you will be treated to some of the finest mountain scenery in the world. From a small alpine town, the red train makes a steep climb up the Jungfrau mountain and past a famous peak called the Eiger. Many climbers died on the sheer north face of the Eiger before it was finally scaled in 1938. The dark, vertical cliff is festooned with trails of ice that give it its nickname, The White Spider.

Moving out of the shadow of the Eiger, the train stops at a station on a high pass that gives amazing views of the mountains all around. The jagged peaks are draped with gleaming glaciers. They are cut by deep cracks and many have knife-edged ridges. Believe it or not, all of these dramatic features were carved by ice.

Like the Himalayas, the Alps are a range of fold mountains formed by uplift and they are still rising. However, even as mountains rise, they are also worn away.

The wearing away of rocks and mountains happens in two stages. The first stage is called weathering, and it happens as the rocks on Earth's surface are exposed to sunshine, frost, and rain. As the water around rocks heats up during the day and freezes at night, the rocks crack and flakes break off. Aided by gravity, the rocky pieces tumble downhill and pile up at the foot of cliffs in heaps called scree.

Sooner or later, most of the rocky fragments blow away in the wind, or are carried off by ice, streams, or rivers. This is the second stage in the process and is called **erosion**.

Weathering and erosion happen at different speeds depending on a region's climate—for example, whether rainfall is high or temperatures are extreme. It also depends on the type of rocks that lie at the surface. Hard rocks such as granite wear away very slowly. Softer ones such as limestone wear away much more quickly. Bare rock faces like the peaks above the pass in Switzerland are eroded more quickly than the rocks of the valley below, which are protected by soil, grass, and trees.

The effects of weathering and erosion on different rocks produce various types of amazing scenery. The soaring peaks of the Alps look fixed and unchanging, but even the hardest rocks are eventually worn away. Millions of years from now, these rugged peaks will be lower and more rounded, just as very ancient mountains are today.

Ice in the form of glaciers is the main force shaping mountains like the Alps. A glacier is a huge mass of ice that moves very slowly downhill. Glaciers are sometimes called "rivers of ice." Like rivers, they flow

downhill, only much more slowly than liquid water.
   Glaciers begin high in the mountains,
in hollows between peaks where snow collects. The
snow builds up and gets squashed by the heavy
layers, which creates ice. Eventually the mass of ice
becomes so big and heavy, it starts to shift downhill.

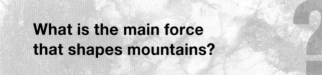

**What is the main force
that shapes mountains?**

Just like water, ice takes the easiest path downhill, flowing down steep-sided gullies cut by streams. The glacier spreads out to fill the narrow valley with ice, which may be hundreds of feet thick. Under pressure from the great weight above, the ice at the base of the glacier melts, forming a trickle of water. This allows the glacier to slide downhill with ease.

As it heads downhill, the huge tongue of ice picks up rocks and boulders on its base and sides. This rocky debris increases erosion, scraping and gouging away at the base. Down in the valley where it is warmer, the ice melts and the glacier ends in a pool of meltwater that feeds fast-flowing streams. The rocky debris carried by the glacier is dumped in giant heaps called moraine.

Ice covers about ten percent of Earth's surface today. The ice-covered areas are made up of glaciers in high mountains and ice caps that cover land in the polar regions. During periods in Earth's history called ice ages, temperatures were generally colder and ice covered more of the planet's surface.

The last ice age lasted from around 30,000 to 10,000 years ago. When it ended, much of the ice in warmer parts of the world melted to reveal landscapes carved by glaciers. As you leave the train station on the high pass and head downhill on foot, you encounter a truly spectacular example of what ice can do to the landscape.

Not far from the pass, the grassy pastures drop away steeply and a great gulf opens up in front of you. Soon you arrive at the rim of an enormous U-shaped valley with almost vertical sides. Waterfalls plunge off the sheer cliffs to drop hundreds of feet to the floor of the flat-bottomed valley far below.

As you head downhill on a steep, zigzagging path, you realize that this enormous valley was once filled with ice. The broad U-shape is proof that this valley was carved by an enormous glacier, which bulldozed its way through here during the last ice age. It transformed a narrow, V-shaped river valley into its present broad, flat-bottomed shape. It is an awesome reminder of the erosive power of ice.

Woolly Mammoth Dug from Siberian Ice

Scientists have discovered the well-preserved remains of a baby woolly mammoth in the Siberian ice.

The baby mammoth that was pulled from the ice last month is one of the best-preserved specimens that has ever been found. It is thought that the baby died 42,000 years ago, when she was sucked into a swamp and buried.

Mammoths disappeared by the end of the last ice age, 10,000 years ago. Ice ages are periods in the Earth's past when the climate was much colder than today. Scientists believe that many ice ages have come and gone in the last two million years. During the last ice age, ice covered much of North America, Europe, Asia, southern South America, and Australia. Ice covered about 30 percent of the planet, compared with just 10 percent today.

The last ice age came to an end because of a rise in the Earth's temperature, which caused most of the ice to melt. This change in the planet's climate led to the loss of habitat for many animals, which caused many species, such as the woolly mammoth, to become extinct. In recent

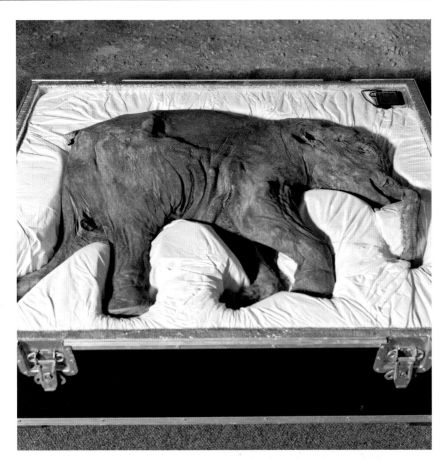

Lyuba was found in the snow by a reindeer herder and his sons.

years, the climate has become even warmer because of human-made pollution.

The young mammoth is an incredible find and will teach us more about her species, what they ate, and how they lived. The mummified animal has been named Lyuba, which means "love" in Russian.

Protecting our Heritage

GALÀPAGOS ISLANDS, SOUTH AMERICA These 19 islands hold an abundance of unique wildlife, such as giant tortoises and marine iguanas.

HA LONG BAY, VIETNAM This gulf includes 1,600 small islands, some of which have been untouched by humans. They form a seascape of limestone pillars.

World Heritage sites are places of special importance as recognized by **UNESCO—the United Nations Educational, Scientific, and Cultural Organization**. They may be places of historical importance, such as an ancient temple or city, or they may be beautiful wild places such as the mountains and glaciers of the Jungfrau region in Switzerland.

SUNDARBANS, SOUTH ASIA This mangrove forest is one of the largest such forests in the world and is home to Bengal tigers and other threatened species.

DINOSAUR PROVINCIAL PARK, CANADA This park contains the remains of some of the most important fossils.

CHAPTER **3**

EARTH'S LONGEST RIVER

Imagine you are in a small plane, flying high above the Nile River in North Africa. The view below you is extraordinary: a bright green ribbon winding through a vast brown landscape stretching to the horizon. This ribbon is a narrow strip of fertile land running along the Nile as it flows through the Sahara Desert. As the plane swoops lower, you can see fields and small towns lining the river. The Nile has transformed this landscape, bringing life to a barren desert.

The Nile is one of the world's greatest rivers. At approximately 4,132 miles (6,650 km) long, it is the world's longest river. The Nile does not carry nearly as much water as rivers such as the Congo in West Africa or the Amazon in South America. This is because it flows through a desert so relatively few rivers join it.

Rivers begin in hills or mountains that receive a lot of rain or snowfall. The water is channeled into streams, which join up to make a river. The main river becomes larger and more powerful as smaller rivers, called tributaries, join it. Pulled by gravity, rivers flow downhill to end in a lake, swamp, or the sea.

A river's course can take it through many different landscapes on its journey. The Nile begins at Lake Victoria in the highlands of East Africa, and flows north to the Mediterranean Sea. On its way, it passes through 11 countries, which it supplies with precious water.

The place where a river begins is called the source. Lake Victoria is unmistakable—a huge body of water bordering Kenya, Tanzania, and Uganda. This is a lake so vast that it looks like a sea.

For a long time, no one knew the source of the Nile, until an explorer called John Speke tracked it to Lake Victoria in 1860. Many streams flowing down from the surrounding hills feed the lake and any one of these could claim to be the true source of the Nile. However, the Nile's length is measured from where it leaves Lake Victoria.

There used to be a huge waterfall where the newborn river left Lake Victoria. The river has now been dammed, closing off the lake. This is just one of many changes that have been made to the river. All along its course, canals, lakes, and **dams** have been built to supply local people with water for drinking and farming, and to generate electricity.

The first part of a river's journey is called the upper course. At this stage, the young Nile flows down from the hills through a narrow gorge, which it has carved through solid rock. Water is one of the most powerful forces of erosion.

Rivers cut down most deeply where they flow over steeply sloping ground or where they pass over soft rocks.

As a fast-flowing river gushes downhill, the water picks up stones and boulders and carries them downstream. This rocky debris is called the river's load. Bouncing along the bed, the debris acts like sandpaper, scraping away more stones and soil, increasing erosion.

As the Nile continues, it becomes a stunning waterfall where it plunges over a sheer cliff. This is Murchison Falls, where the river drops 141 ft (43 m). Waterfalls form where a river flows from hard rocks onto softer rocks. The soft rocks erode to leave a cliff over which the river plunges. The cascading water carves a deep pool at the base. Meanwhile stones and boulders, carried along by the river's current, gradually break up to form fine **sediment**, called silt.

Heading northward, the Nile enters a huge swamp called the Sudd. These green wetlands are home to hippos, crocodiles, and herons. The river slows, and much of its water **evaporates** in the hot sunlight. Farther downstream, near the city of Khartoum in Sudan, the clear blue waters of another river join the brownish waters of the Nile.

A place where two rivers meet is called a confluence. The clear waters are the Blue Nile, which rises far to the east in the highlands of Ethiopia. The river from Lake Victoria is called the White Nile—it is brown and murky because it contains so much sediment. From here on, the river is simply called the Nile.

Beyond Khartoum, the Nile meanders in a great loop and passes over several **cataracts**, where the foaming water churns over large boulders in its riverbed. Continuing north, the river enters a long, thin lake called Lake Nasser. The building of the giant Aswan Dam in 1970 formed this artificial lake. The dam was built to control the river flow and to generate electricity for Egypt.

Before the dam was built, the Nile used to burst its banks in the rainy season and flood the surrounding land. Rich **silt** dropped by the flooding created fertile farmland. One of the world's earliest civilizations grew up along the river and ancient Egyptian farmers grew several crops a year in the rich silt. Since the Aswan Dam was built, the river no longer floods and modern farmers have to use artificial fertilizers to nourish the soil.

At Aswan, the lower course of the river continues toward the sea. Small boats with triangular sails called feluccas have been sailing the Nile for thousands of years. As the feluccas head north, the city of Luxor, with its amazing temples, comes into view. On the west bank of the Nile is the famous Valley of the Kings, where the Egyptian pharaohs were buried. These kings were buried with fabulous treasure, but almost all of it was looted long ago. However, in 1922 **archaeologist** Howard Carter discovered the tomb of the boy-king Tutankhamun. It had never been robbed and was filled to the brim with golden treasure.

Sailing onward, farther north is the vast city of Cairo. The famous pyramids nearby date back 5,000 years. They were built using huge limestone blocks carried along the Nile by **barge**. Without the river, these magnificent structures could never have been built.

Beyond Cairo, the river flows through a flat plain to the sea. As it reaches the Mediterranean, the current slows abruptly. The sluggish water no longer has the energy to carry sediment. Silt dropped by the river has formed a large, fan-shaped area called a delta. The land here is very fertile. The Nile splits into many smaller channels as it completes its long journey, and its fresh waters mingle with the salty sea.

Waterfalls

What are they?

A waterfall is a torrent of water that falls from a great height, usually over a steep drop.

How do they form?

- Waterfalls can be created by erosion.
- The force of the water in a river or stream erodes the soft rock that it flows across.
- When the soft rock is worn away, it leaves a hard, unsupported ledge that the water tumbles over.
- Over time, the cascading water undercuts the hard rock. The rock collapses, sending the rocks crashing into a plunge pool below.
- This process is repeated and the waterfall becomes bigger and bigger.

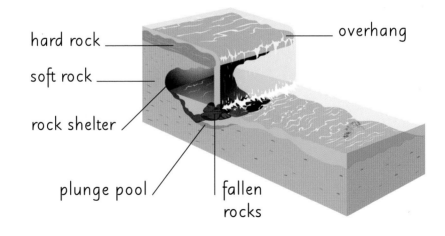

hard rock

soft rock

rock shelter

plunge pool

overhang

fallen rocks

VICTORIA FALLS in Africa is one of the world's loudest waterfalls. The thick mist and loud noise produced by it can be seen and heard up to 25 miles (40 km) away. Local people call the falls Mosi-oa-Tunya, or "The Smoke that Thunders."

RECORD BREAKERS
Angel Falls in Venezuela is the highest waterfall in the world. It plunges 3,212 ft (980 m) into the Kerep River below.

NIAGARA FALLS on the border between the USA and Canada, has the fastest water flow. The river plunges 188 ft (57 m) and the flow is fastest in the center, where the rocks have worn away more quickly to form a giant horseshoe.

CHAPTER **4**

CHANGING COASTS

One afternoon in July 2005, a bus arrived on the south coast of Australia. A group of tourists and their guide got out, walked to the cliff edge and looked over. They had come to see the Twelve Apostles, a magnificent group of rock pillars standing in the water just offshore. Named after the twelve original followers of Jesus, the rock stacks are a popular attraction. Thousands come to photograph the limestone pillars, which glow deep yellow in the evening sun. When the stacks came into view, the guide immediately noticed something was different—one Apostle was missing! One of the tall pillars had collapsed, leaving just a heap of rocks stranded in the sea.

The collapse of the Australian Apostle is just one example of how coastal scenery all over the world is constantly changing. Coasts form the border between the dry land and the ocean, and this strip of land is a battleground between solid rock and the forces of erosion: powerful winds and crashing waves.

More than 530,000 miles (853,000 km) of coastline edge Earth's continents and islands. The scenery found at the coasts varies greatly—there may be high cliffs, rugged headlands, or sand or pebble beaches. Where rivers meet the sea, salt marshes, mudflats, and swampy deltas are found and huge blocks of floating ice line the coasts in the polar regions. Whatever the scenery, however, coasts never look the same for very long.

Every minute of every day, waves wash against the shore. When the weather is calm, this is just a gentle lapping, but in gales and storms, foaming breakers smash against the coast with tremendous force. Waves fling grit, sand, and pebbles against the rocks.

Under this continuous battering, coastal rocks crack, then cracks widen and flakes break off. Every year, waves remove several inches of rock from the bases of the Twelve Apostles. Over time, erosion makes the rocks top-heavy, and eventually a whole stack collapses, as happened on that day in 2005. Powerful currents also flow along many coasts, adding to the attack on coastal rocks.

As if the buffeting of the waves were not enough, the sea also rushes high up the shore twice a day, and then falls back again. These changes in sea level are called tides, and they are caused by the tug of the Moon's **gravity** on the oceans.

Just as on land, the speed of erosion on coasts is affected by the type of rocks being worn away. Soft rocks such as chalk wear away much more quickly than hard rocks such as granite. Waves will wear away soft rocks on the coastline to form wide, curving bays or deep indents, called coves.

Hard rocks at the coast wear away more slowly, leaving rugged **headlands** jutting out to sea. But sooner or later, even the hardest rocks give way to the waves. Where waves curve around a headland, they carve deep caves. Caves on either side of a headland may eventually wear all the way through to form an arch. As erosion continues, the top of the arch may collapse, leaving rock pillars, like the Twelve Apostles, standing in the ocean.

Cliffs are found on coasts wherever high ground meets the ocean. The cliffs behind the Twelve Apostles rise 230 ft (70 m), but some cliffs are much taller—the very tallest towers over 3,300 ft (1,000 m) above the ocean.

As waves strike the bases of cliffs, they wear a deep groove into the stone. Eventually the rock on top collapses, and the coast moves inland. The stacks of the Twelve Apostles mark the line where the land once ended and the ocean began. The present cliffs lie several hundred feet inland, but the ocean is still eating away at their bases, forming new caves and arches. The land is gradually retreating. Some coasts are shifting inland by more than 3 ft (1 m) a year.

The ocean doesn't only wear away the land—in some places, it also helps build it. Waves, tides, and currents carry rocky debris that was worn from cliffs and washed out to sea by rivers. Out in the open water, waves have the energy to shift huge amounts of debris, but in sheltered bays and coves the current weakens. The rocky debris gets dumped, and if it stays out at sea, it may build up to form an island. If it washes ashore, it forms a beach. This process is called deposition. However, loose sand, stones, or pebbles on a beach are at risk of erosion. Violent storms can shift sand along a beach, or even wash it away completely.

In warm, shallow waters in the tropics, you find a very different type of coastal scenery—coral reefs. These reefs may lie just offshore or form a barrier farther out at sea. Coral reefs resemble rocks, but they are actually built by small sea creatures called coral polyps, which live in large groups called colonies.

Coral polyps are related to sea anemones. Like anemones, they have a soft, tube-shaped body with a crown of tentacles on top. The tentacles waft in the current and capture the polyp's food. The base of the soft body is protected by a chalky cup that is anchored to the reef. When the polyp dies the soft parts rot quickly, but the stony cup remains. New polyps grow on top, so the reef grows bigger very slowly. However, like all coastal features, coral reefs are at risk of erosion. Chunks of coral can be broken off by crashing waves, especially during storms.

GALLERY OF FAMOUS COASTAL FEATURES

A coast is where the land meets the ocean. Coastlines are formed and broken down in many different ways. Processes that can change the shape of coasts include: the flow of glaciers, lava, sediment, waves, tides, currents, and changing sea levels.

SPOUTING HORN, HAWAII

This coastal phenomenon occurs when water rushes under a shelf of dried lava and shoots through a small opening on the surface.

DURDLE DOOR, ENGLAND

A remnant of a once-large cliff, this limestone arch was formed when the crashing waves eroded away the soft rock in the center, leaving a hard stone arch behind.

DUNGENESS SPIT, WASHINGTON, USA

This 5.5 mile (9 km) stretch of sand was created by deposition—when sand and stones are washed along the coast and deposited in the sea, forming long, thin islands.

OREGON DUNES

These sand dunes were formed by erosion and the transport of sand by ocean winds. The process has taken millions of years and the winds still continue to mold the sand dunes into wavelike shapes today.

Coasts Under Attack!

Sea defenses urgently needed!

ATTENTION ALL DEFENDERS OF THE COASTS!

We're here to protect our coastline and we need to make sure we do a very good job. It's time for us to put our words into action to save the world's beaches!

Seaside towns the world over are being invaded by the ocean and we will not rest until it is beaten! Climate change is causing our planet to overheat, the polar ice to melt, and the sea levels to rise. Storms and high tides are threatening to swamp cities and farmland, and whole island nations could disappear beneath the waves if we don't do our best to help them.

Our first lines of defense are to put boulders on the beaches to reduce the strength of the waves. Then we will make breakwaters to protect ports from the raging seas. Where waves strike the shore at an angle, they are transporting sand along the beach. To combat this, we will be building fences called groins to help keep the sand in place.

Stay strong and defend your land. No matter what the seas throw our way, we must be ready!

JOIN US TODAY!

CHAPTER **5**

WIND-SCOURED DESERTS

It is dawn in the Canyonlands of North America, hundreds of years ago. Two figures stand under an enormous stone arch, looking out over a dry, rocky landscape. As the sun rises, the rugged cliffs glow rosy red, then flush bright orange. The shadow of the great arch creeps across the canyon, which is dotted with sagebrush. The pair often come here before dawn, leaving their cliff dwelling, or pueblo, to pay their respects to their ancestors and pray for good hunting.

The pictures of animals etched into nearby rocks show that their people have been doing the same for hundreds of years.

This rock arch, which was a sacred site for Anasazi or ancestral Puebloans, who were Native American peoples centuries ago, now stands in Arches National Park in southwestern USA. The park holds hundreds of amazing rock formations. As well as delicate rock arches, which resemble rainbows turned to stone, there are tall, slender spires of rock, and huge boulders perched on narrow columns. These extraordinary formations were carved into the sandstone by the elements—sunshine, ice, and wind.

Spectacular rock formations are common in deserts because there are few plants and little soil to protect the rocks from the weather. Deserts are found on every continent on Earth. The vast, snow-covered continent of Antarctica is a desert because so little rain falls there.

Deserts experience some of the harshest conditions on the planet. Not far from Arches National Park lies Death Valley—North America's driest desert. This is one of the hottest places on Earth, with temperatures rising to a sizzling

134°F (57°C). However, not all deserts are hot—some are icy cold, especially in winter.

What all deserts have in common is a lack of water. If an area receives less than 10 inches (25 cm) of rain a year, we call it a desert. Deserts are dry because there are no clouds to bring rain. Many of the world's deserts lie 10–30° north and south of the equator. Here the air is warm and dry, so no clouds can form. Other deserts lie near the center of continents, away from the moisture-laden winds that blow in from the oceans.

Most deserts are scorching hot by day because there are no clouds to screen the fierce sunlight. But at night, temperatures plunge below zero because there are no clouds to keep in the heat.

Extremes of temperature in deserts cause weathering, which has helped sculpt the arches and pinnacles that can be seen at Arches National Park. By day, rocks expand in the heat, but then contract (get smaller) in the chill of night.

The constant expansion and contraction weakens rocks. The outer layers can peel away like the skin of an onion. Fine cracks also develop in rock slabs. The dew that falls as temperatures drop at sunset trickles into cracks, and then the moisture expands as it freezes into ice. This widens the cracks until, eventually, rocks shatter, and the loose pieces fall away.

Wind is a powerful erosive force in deserts. Small pieces of grit and fine sand are picked up by the wind and blown along at low level, a couple of feet above the ground. Grit and sand carried by the wind act like sandpaper, scouring away at rock faces. This creates smooth, rounded shapes and also undercuts rocks, to form top-heavy pillars called hoodoos. In some places, narrow fins of rock, formed by weathering, are worn through to form graceful arches. For years these can seem to defy gravity, but eventually as erosion continues, the delicate shapes come crashing down.

In some deserts, huge quantities of sand have collected to form sand dunes. If winds blow mainly from one direction, they can sculpt the loose sand into crescent-shaped heaps called barchan dunes, or into long, straight ridges called seif dunes. Strong gusts can scoop up sand and fling it high into the air, to create sandstorms and whirlwinds.

Deserts may endure parched conditions for many years, but when rain does at last fall, usually in a **cloudburst**, the ground is too dry to absorb it. Torrential rain pours away into dry gullies, carrying stones and boulders along with it. This adds to the scouring of desert landscapes, and helps shape the dramatic features that can be seen in these dry places today.

Extreme Desert Survival

with Freddie Fennec

Welcome to *Extreme Desert Survival*

I'm Freddie Fennec and today we are going to be searching the world's deserts for some of the toughest animals that live in this scorching and unforgiving habitat.

The sun has just begun to rise over the desert and here we can see a tortoise that has joined us to warm its shell. This animal spends 95 percent of its life in burrows underground, in order to escape the searing heat.

Here we have a shovel-snouted lizard. This reptile is able to withstand very high temperatures, but when things do become a bit too warm underfoot, it will hop up and down in a unique dance. By keeping two feet off the sand at any time it can cool itself down.

Many desert animals only venture out at night when it is cooler. We have waited until the dead of night to find a rattlesnake catching its prey. Rattlesnakes can hunt in pitch-darkness, thanks to heat-sensing "pits" on their heads.

This scorpion also hunts at night and will lie in wait to catch its prey using its pincers. If its prey is especially feisty, the scorpion can also paralyze it using the venom in its stinger.

ULURU Tourist Board

AYERS ROCK

ULURU, ALSO KNOWN AS AYERS ROCK,
is one of the most famous sights in Australia.
This extraordinary rock outcrop rises 1,141 ft
(348 m) above a red, dusty plain in the
center of Australia. As the world's largest
monolith (single block of rock), it is a sacred
site for Aboriginal peoples.

This massive rock is made of sandstone, laid
down as sand 500 million years ago. Squashed
by more sediment, the sand turned to rock, and
later plate movements tilted the rock layers.
Extreme temperatures, wind, and water have
worn deep grooves in the rock.

HOW TO GET THERE
Fly into Ayers Rock Airport, or land at Alice Springs, and rent a car or take the bus. The 280-mile (450-km) trip takes about five hours.

WHERE TO STAY
You will need several days to explore Uluru and nearby sights. The Ayers Rock Resort has accommodation of all kinds, from campsites to luxury hotels.

THINGS TO DO
☆ The best time to view Uluru is at sunrise or sunset, when the rock glows deep red.
☆ Complete the 5-mile (9-km) circuit of Uluru on foot, camel, bike, or motorcycle.
☆ Local guides can be on hand to explain the rock's history, culture, and wildlife.
☆ Explore the extraordinary landscapes nearby: Kata Tjuta (The Olgas) and Kings Canyon.

The Anangu Australian Aborigines officially own the area and it has great cultural and traditional meaning to them.

CHAPTER **6**

THE GRAND CANYON

An inflatable raft pulls away from the bank and glides swiftly downstream. Sheer rock walls, in shades of pink and yellow, rise hundreds of feet above the green river. The raft slides past rocks worn smooth and glossy by the river, and leafy canyon walls with cascading waterfalls. At first the water swirls gently, but there is **white water** downstream, and soon the raft hits the rapids! The raft rears and pitches like a bucking horse. The passengers are drenched by spray and deafened by the roaring water. But the oarsman guides the raft safely through to calm water. The scenery on all sides is breathtaking. This is the Colorado River winding through the Grand Canyon—a trip that will never be forgotten.

The Grand Canyon is one of North America's greatest wonders. This vast canyon carved by the Colorado River is 277 miles (446 km) long, over 1 mile (1.6 km) deep, and up to 18 miles (29 km) wide. It is one of Earth's very largest, longest, and deepest **gorges**.

The Colorado River meanders eastward, cutting down through a high, rocky plateau. The deep gorge cut by the river is so wide that the two canyon rims sometimes have very different weather. The rugged North Rim may be hit by a thunderstorm while the lower South Rim is bathed in sunshine.

This plateau is actually younger than the river flowing through it. This is because this awe-inspiring feature was created by two powerful forces: fast-flowing water and uplift, the force that builds mountains.

Six million years ago, the young river meandered though a low-lying plain, and the scenery was a lot less spectacular than today. As tectonic plates shifted, the land was forced upward to form a high plateau and as the land rose, the river continued to cut downward. In fact, as the slopes became steeper, the water flowed faster and carved into the rocks more quickly. Erosion still continues, so the canyon is getting deeper as the river carves away at its riverbed.

As the Colorado has cut downward, it has revealed layers of limestone, sandstone, and shale. Millions of years ago, these rocks settled as sediment, either on the bed of shallow seas or in sandy deserts. The sediment was squashed and buried beneath more layers of sand and mud, and slowly hardened into stone.

Rocks that form in this way are called sedimentary rocks. Later these layers of rock were uplifted and then eroded by the river. As elsewhere, soft rocks wore away more quickly than hard ones. This has created the stepped sides of the canyon. The layering

of rock has produced bands of color on the sheer walls: creamy limestone, red sandstone, gray shale, and pink granite.

Since the rocks settled in horizontal layers, the ones at the bottom are the oldest. The rocks down by the river are incredibly ancient—up to two billion years old—but the rocks up at the rim are much younger at only 250 million years old. This means that if you stand on the rim and look down, you are gazing into Earth's distant history—a time long before humans, mammals, and even dinosaurs existed.

Every year, the Grand Canyon receives approximately five million visitors and the area is now protected as a national park. Native Americans have lived in the region for thousands of years and in 1869, an American soldier named John Wesley Powell led an expedition to explore the canyon by boat.

In 1903, US President Theodore Roosevelt

visited the Grand Canyon. This was in the early days of conservation, when people were beginning to understand the importance of protecting wild places. Thanks to Roosevelt, the Grand Canyon became a national monument in 1908, and then a national park in 1919. The president wrote: "Leave it as it is. You cannot improve on it. The ages have been at work on it and man can only **mar** it. What you can do is keep it for your children [and] your children's children...."

Today, in addition to rafting, visitors can hike to the bottom of the canyon or ride down on a mule. Most people stay at the top, driving around the rim and stopping to admire the view. In 2007, the park opened a glass-bottomed bridge, called the Skywalk, which allows tourists to gaze directly down at the river 4,000 ft (1,219 m) below.

How do sedimentary rocks form?

Grand Canyon National Park, just like other parks all over the world, has two main aims: to protect nature and to allow people to enjoy it. Sometimes these two aims conflict with each other. Tourists need places to eat, stay, and buy souvenirs, so the authorities must provide hotels, campsites, parking lots, stores, and restaurants. At the same time, they must ensure that this development does not spoil the very beauty people come to see.

Tourists in large numbers can harm nature by dropping litter, eroding paths, disturbing wildlife, and causing air pollution. National parks have strict rules to protect nature, for example, no one is allowed to pick flowers or disturb the animals. Their motto is, "Take nothing but pictures. Leave nothing but footprints." Thanks to the authorities, amazing landscapes like the Grand Canyon are being preserved for the future, so people can enjoy them for many years to come.

MAJOR
JOHN WESLEY POWELL
Exploring the Grand Canyon

On May 24, 1869, Major John Wesley Powell led the first expedition to explore the Grand Canyon by river. Ten men set off in four boats laden with supplies. Powell aimed to map the canyon and study its rocks and wildlife. He was an expert geologist, who had fought and lost one arm in the American Civil War.

Floating swiftly downstream, the expedition entered the canyon. Sheer walls of rock rose high above them. No one knew what challenges lay ahead. The men listened for the telltale roar of a waterfall that could sweep them to their deaths if they were not careful. In his diary Powell wrote,

"We have an unknown distance yet to run.... What falls there are, we know not; what rocks beset the channel, we know not; what walls ride over the river, we know not."

The expedition had to pass hundreds of dangerous rapids, which one man described as "a perfect hell of waves." The men had to cling on to their boats to avoid drowning. On the worst stretches, the men lifted the boats out of the river and lugged everything along the bank to calmer water. At night, they camped on the sandy beaches. Powell took measurements, collected rock samples, and several times climbed the sheer walls to the rim of the canyon—and he managed it all with just one arm!

By August 28, the men were starving. Two boats had been lost, along with much of the food and one man had already deserted the team. Now three other men decided to leave the expedition—to climb to the rim of the canyon and hike out through the desert. They were never seen again. However, just two days later, the boats cleared the end of the canyon and to everyone's delight, reached safety. Powell became famous. After his journey, he campaigned for conservation of the canyon and for the rights of the Native Americans who lived there.

Birds of the Grand Canyon

Are you an eagle-eyed bird watcher? Then head to the Grand Canyon this fall to see if you can find a falcon or spy a hawk flying over one of the world's most iconic landscapes.

How to be a pro birdwatcher

✔ Use high-powered binoculars to see birds from far away.

✔ Take notes of what birds you see—write down any special markings, unusual plumage, or how their call sounds.

✔ Remember that the safety of the birds comes first—do not try to chase or catch them.

Birds to keep an eye out for

✔ Golden and Bald eagles

✔ Hawks

✔ Kestrels

✔ Peregrine falcons

✔ California condors

Bald Eagle

SIZE: 28–38 in. (71–96 cm) long   DIET: mainly fish
HABITAT: near rivers, lakes, and on coasts
DISTRIBUTION: North America

The Bald Eagle is the national bird of the USA. Bald eagles use their talons to snatch fish out of the water to eat. They are also scavengers and often steal food from other birds. These birds mate for life and construct enormous nests to lay their eggs in.

Peregrine Falcon

SIZE: 13.5–23 in. (34–58 cm) long   DIET: mainly birds
HABITAT: nests on rock ledges
DISTRIBUTION: worldwide, except Antarctica

Peregrine Falcons are the world's fastest birds. Falcons are effective hunters and can spot prey from high up in the sky, swooping down at speeds of up to 200 mph (325 kph). The name "peregrine" means "wanderer" because many falcons migrate south, to warmer climates, for the winter months.

Big Fantastic Earth Quiz

See if you can remember the answers to these questions about what you have read.

1. Who were the first people to set foot on the top of Everest?

2. What are mountains formed by plate collisions called?

3. What is the name for a mass of ice that moves slowly downhill?

4. What is the world's longest river called?

5. What is the name of the place where a river begins?

6. Are hard or soft rocks eroded more quickly?

7. Why was the Aswan Dam built?

8. Where is the highest waterfall in the world?

9. What force causes tides in the sea?

10. What is the name of the process that forms beaches?

11. What do coral polyps form?

12. Antarctica is a desert: true or false?

13. What is the other name for Ayers Rock?

14. What is the name of the American soldier who explored the Grand Canyon by boat in 1869?

15. What river winds through the Grand Canyon?

Answers on page 93.

Glossary

Archaeologist
A person who studies human history by uncovering and finding human remains and objects.

Barge
Flat-bottomed boat built for transport of heavy goods along rivers and canals.

Cataracts
White water rapids in the Nile River.

Cloudburst
Sudden rainstorm.

Dam
Barrier that holds back water.

Equator
Imaginary line around the middle of the Earth that divides it into the northern and southern hemispheres.

Erosion
When elements such as water or wind wears away and removes soil or rock.

Evaporates
When something turns from a liquid into a gas, for example when water is heated it becomes water vapor.

Gorge
Steep-sided narrow valley often with a stream running through it.

Gravity
Force that causes objects to fall towards the center of a planet or moon.

Headlands
Sections of land that jut out towards the sea.

Mar
Spoil.

Sediment
Material that settles at the bottom of a river or ocean.

Silt
Grainy material made of minerals that is similar to sand or clay.

White water
Fast flowing stretches of water in a river.

Answers to the Big Fantastic Earth Quiz:
1. Edmund Hillary and Tenzing Norgay; **2.** Fold mountains; **3.** Glacier; **4.** The Nile; **5.** The source; **6.** Soft rocks; **7.** To control the river flow and to generate electricity for Egypt; **8.** Angel Falls in Venezuela; **9.** Gravity; **10.** Deposition; **11.** Coral reefs; **12.** True; **13.** Uluru; **14.** Major John Wesley Powell; **15.** Colorado River.

Guide for Parents

DK Readers is a four-level interactive reading adventure series for children, developing the habit of reading widely for both pleasure and information. These books have an exciting main narrative interspersed with a range of reading genres to suit your child's reading ability. Each book is designed to develop your child's reading skills, fluency, grammar awareness, and comprehension in order to build confidence and engagement when reading.

Ready for a *Reading Alone* book

YOUR CHILD SHOULD

- be able to read independently and silently for extended periods of time.
- read aloud flexibly and fluently, in expressive phrases with the listener in mind.
- be able to respond to what is being read and be able to discuss key ideas in the text.

A VALUABLE AND SHARED READING EXPERIENCE

Supporting children when they are reading proficiently can encourage them to value reading and to view reading as an interesting, purposeful, and enjoyable pastime. So here are a few tips on how to use this book with your child.

TIP 1 Reading aloud as a learning opportunity:

- after your child has read a part of the book, ask him/her to tell you what has happened so far.
- even though your child may be reading independently, most children at this level still enjoy having a parent read aloud. Take turns reading sections of the book, especially sections that contain dialogue that can provide practice in expressive reading.

TIP 2 Chat at the end of each chapter:

- encourage your child to recall specific details after each chapter.
- let your child pick out interesting words and discuss what they mean.
- talk about what each of you found most interesting or most important.
- ask the questions provided on some pages and in the quiz. These help to develop comprehension skills and awareness of the language used.
- ask if there's anything that your child would like to discover more about.

Further information can be researched in the index of other nonfiction books or on the Internet.

A FEW ADDITIONAL TIPS

- Continue to read to your child regularly to demonstrate fluency, phrasing and expression; to find out or check information; and for sharing enjoyment.
- Encourage your child to read a range of different genres, such as newspapers, poems, review articles and instructions.
- Provide opportunities for your child to read to a variety of eager listeners, such as a sibling or a grandparent.

Series consultant, **Dr. Linda Gambrell**, Distinguished Professor of Education at Clemson University, has served as President of the National Reading Conference, the College Reading Association, and the International Reading Association.

Index